Gu
Lan
Pub

Nick Burton

Pendle Hill

COUNTRYSIDE BOOKS
NEWBURY BERKSHIRE

First published 2018
Text © 2018 Nick Burton

COUNTRYSIDE BOOKS
3 Catherine Road
Newbury, Berkshire

To view our complete range of books,
please visit us at
www.countrysidebooks.co.uk

ISBN 978 1 84674 364 1

Designed by KT Designs, St Helens
Produced through The Letterworks Ltd., Reading
Typeset by KT Designs, St Helens
Printed in Poland

Introduction

The best way to explore Lancashire is undoubtedly on foot. History, landscape, wildlife, and surprising views are all revealed in this series of walks: from the devil's stone head near Ribchester and the Alfred Wainwright viewpoint above Pleasington to the stunning Halo sculpture above Haslingden and the ruins of Hollinshead Hall in the woods below Tockholes. I never tire of walking in my home county as there is always something new to see. In compiling this collection of walks I was particularly drawn to rediscovering again the county's canals and rivers. The walks include excursions along the Lancaster Canal and the Leeds & Liverpool Canal and along the county's major rivers – the Ribble, Lune and Wyre. But I am always drawn towards exploring Lancashire's lesser-known water courses. In completing these walks you will get to know rivers like the Keer, the Tawd, the Calder, the Douglas and the Darwen. As for the views, climb up any of the hill slopes visited in these walks and

The Parkers Arms, Newton

on a good day you can usually see something rewarding. Like Blackpool Tower and the Irish Sea, the Lake District Fells, Bowland, Longridge Fell and Pendle Hill, the West Pennine Moors and, if you are lucky, the Great Orme or even the mountains of Snowdonia. If you add a pint or two of real ale in a village pub at the end of a ramble, I come to the happy conclusion that walking in Lancashire is difficult to beat.

Nick Burton

Publisher's Note

We hope that you obtain considerable enjoyment from this book: great care has been taken in its preparation. However, changes of landlord and actual pub closures are sadly not uncommon. Likewise, although at the time of publication all routes followed public rights of way or permitted paths, diversion orders can be made and permissions withdrawn.

In order to assist in navigation to the start point of the walk, we have included the nearest postcode, although of course a postcode cannot always deliver you to a precise starting point, especially in rural areas.

We cannot, of course, be held responsible for such diversion orders or any inaccuracies in the text which result from these or any other changes to the routes, nor any damage which might result from walkers trespassing on private property. We are anxious, though, that all details covering the walks and the pubs are kept up to date, and would therefore welcome information from readers which would be relevant to future editions.

The simple sketch maps that accompany the walks in this book are based on notes made by the author whilst surveying the routes on the ground. They are designed to show you how to reach the start and to point out the main features of the overall circuit, and they contain a progression of numbers that relate to the paragraphs of the text.

However, for the benefit of a proper map, we do recommend that you purchase the relevant Ordnance Survey sheet covering your walk. Ordnance Survey maps are widely available, especially through booksellers and local newsagents.

Boats on the Lancaster Canal

1 Tewitfield
4 miles / 6.4 km

WALK HIGHLIGHTS
The walk takes in several historic crossing points of the River Keer at Capernwray – the viaduct carrying the Carnforth to Leeds railway line, a packhorse bridge and the Keer Aqueduct carrying the Lancaster Canal 35ft above the river.

THE PUB
The Longlands Hotel, LA6 1JH
☎ 01524 781256 www.longlandshotel.co.uk

THE WALK
Turn left and leave the car park on the opposite side to the hotel, through the gateway signed as '**Canal Walk**'. This leads to the end of the canal next to the M6. Turn left and follow the towpath under several bridges for about one mile, heading south. Leave the canal after passing under bridge number 134.

Leave it on the right, climbing the stone steps to the bridge. Turn left and follow a track downhill straight ahead. At a track junction, turn left

HOW TO GET THERE AND PARKING: Tewitfield is 1 mile north of junction 35 of the M6. Follow the A6 north from Carnforth and J35 and turn right along the A6070 at the Pine Lakes roundabout. Follow this for ¾ mile, cross over the M6, and Tewitfield Marina is on the right-hand side adjacent to the Longlands Hotel, where there is a large car park. **Sat nav** LA6 1JH.

MAP: OS Explorer OL7 The English Lakes South Eastern area. **Grid ref** SD 520737.

and continue along the hedged track. Fork left and the path goes under a railway viaduct. Cross the little bridge over the **River Keer** and walk straight ahead up a track to meet a lane.

❸ Turn left along the lane and cross canal bridge number 131. Turn left at the footpath signpost following the drive into the **New England Caravan Park**. Cross over the **Keer Aqueduct** high above the river. Follow the driveway under the railway bridge and keep left between two stone walls. Keep to the canalside path to reach the far side of the caravan park. Fork left at a waymarker post, heading for trees.

❹ At the woodland edge, the path forks into two. Take the right fork through the woodland and the path climbs uphill as a sunken path around the back of an old quarry on the right. Reach a stile on the left by the caravan site gate.

❺ Cross the stile, aiming diagonally right to the opposite corner of the field. In the right-hand corner the field becomes a narrow strip between hedges leading to a squeeze stile in a wall. Cross further wall stiles keeping to the left-hand side of fields to eventually cross a stile to a lane. Turn left and follow the lane uphill for about half a mile to reach the phone box by the village green overlooked by **Borwick Hall**.

❻ Turn right at the phone box along the lane signed for **Priest Hutton**. Keep right on the adjoining lane and, when it bends right, leave it along the signed footpath to the left of **Rosethorn Cottage**. This goes through a gateway between houses to reach a field gate. Do not go through this but turn right at the waymarked fence post. The path runs between a hedge and farm wall. Go through another gateway and stile keeping above farm buildings. Cross a scrubby area and a stile leads into a field. Immediately cross the stile on the left leading into a higher field.

Aim diagonally right uphill across this next field. Go through the squeeze stile between the two gates on the far side of the field. Cross a squeeze stile in the left corner of the next field then follow the next left field edge to cross a stile and meet a hedged track (**Kirkgate Lane**). Turn left and follow this over a hill to meet a lane by a **Methodist chapel**. Turn right along the lane here to reach the **Longlands Hotel**. Alternatively, to avoid the lane, turn left over the canal bridge and join the towpath again, turn left under the bridge to retrace the route to the marina.

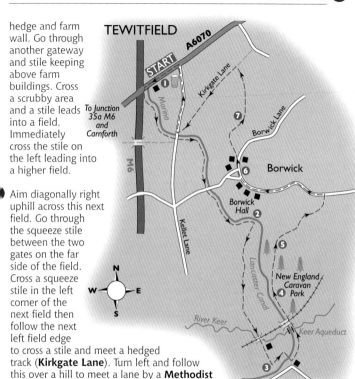

PLACES OF INTEREST NEARBY

Leighton Moss Nature Reserve is a flagship RSPB reserve located just a few miles away (www.rspb.org.uk).

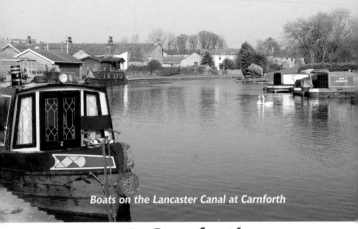
Boats on the Lancaster Canal at Carnforth

2 Carnforth
4 miles / 6.4 km

WALK HIGHLIGHTS

Carnforth's industrial growth had much to do with the ironworks and its importance as a railway junction in the 19th century. This walk follows a section of an earlier transport artery that helped the town develop, the Lancaster Canal, built in the 1790s. The canal brought coal from the south of the county to Lancashire and, in return, limestone and fish from the coastal villages could be transported down to Preston and beyond. The walk route links Carnforth with the Domesday Book fishing village of Bolton-le-Sands. The tracks above the canal offer extensive views northwards across Morecambe Bay to Warton Crag and the Lakeland Fells.

THE PUB
The Canal Turn, LA5 9EA
☎ 01524 720546 www.thecanalturn.co.uk

THE WALK

1 Join the towpath of the **Lancaster Canal** between the **Canal Turn** pub and the petrol station. Turn right along the towpath and follow it in the

HOW TO GET THERE AND PARKING: Carnforth is situated along the A6 close to Junction 35a of the M6 motorway. Follow signs for the town centre and the Canal Turn pub is on the main A6 Lancaster Road on the south (Lancaster) side of the town's main crossroads near to Tesco and next to a petrol station. The pub car park is for patrons only. There is roadside parking on residential streets nearby or alternatively park at the train station in the town centre and start the walk from there. Please note supermarket car parks are for customers only and limited to a maximum of two hours. **Sat nav** LA5 9EA.

MAP: OS Explorer 296 Lancaster, Morecambe & Fleetwood and OS Explorer OL7 English Lakes South-eastern area. **Grid ref** SD 495701.

direction of Lancaster. Follow it for about half a mile and it is joined on the right by the A6 close to the first bridge reached over the canal. Leave the towpath at the bridge by turning right through a gate, then left to cross over the bridge. At the junction of tracks on the far side of the bridge, turn right along the access track running alongside the canal now on the right.

Ignore the path forking right alongside the water's edge but keep to the track which climbs uphill away from the canal. The track, known as **Mount Pleasant Lane**, is followed straight ahead for three quarters of a mile, passing **Mount Pleasant Farm** on the right to meet a crossroads of tracks. Continue straight ahead here along a lane that passes through woodland. It is followed for three quarters of a mile past the crossroads and drops gradually downhill to meet a lane by a school. Turn right along the adjoining lane (**Bolton Lane**) and it leads into the village of **Bolton-le-Sands** soon reaching the main street near to the **Blue Anchor** pub.

Turn right along the main village street passing the **Packet Boat** pub on the right. At the road bridge over the Lancaster Canal cross it and join the canal towpath on the left via the steps. Turn left under the bridge and follow the canal for nearly three quarters of a mile. Pass under one bridge and, at the approach to the second bridge, leave it via the gate on the left.

Guide to Lancashire Pub Walks

4 Turn right and cross the canal bridge, passing the entrance to **Thwaite Brow Woods** on the right. Keep to the lane (**Thwaite Brow Lane**) which climbs gradually uphill past houses to reveal good views over to **Warton Crag** and the sands of **Morecambe Bay**. When the lane ends at iron gates, fork left along a grassy path next to a hedge. The path runs along the hillside and drops down to meet the canal on the left. Follow the canalside path back to the bridge crossed near the start of the walk. Turn left over the bridge, then right to join the towpath again. Turn left along the towpath to retrace the walk route back to Carnforth.

PLACES OF INTEREST NEARBY

At the **Carnforth Station Heritage Centre** there are collections of railway memorabilia recording the nostalgic days of steam together with a *Brief Encounter* exhibition dedicated to the classic 1940s David Lean movie which was filmed here (www.carnforthstation.co.uk).

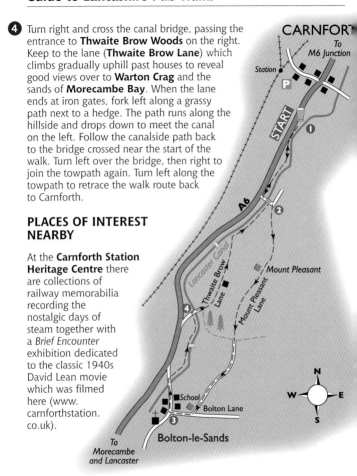

10

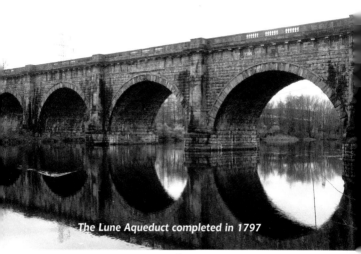

The Lune Aqueduct completed in 1797

3 Halton

3 miles / 4.8 km

WALK HIGHLIGHTS

The mature and mighty River Lune dominates the historic village of Halton, perched on the north side of the river. The river brought industry to Halton in the 18th and 19th centuries with forges, mills and even a stop on the 'Little' North Western Railway, running on the south side of the river from Yorkshire to Lancaster and Morecambe. The redundant station at Halton has been preserved whilst part of the old railway line has been reborn as the popular Lune Valley cycleway. In addition to the road crossings of the Lune at Halton, the most impressive engineering feature is the Lune Aqueduct, completed in 1797, which carries the Lancaster Canal high over the river.

THE PUB

The Greyhound, LA2 6LZ

☎ 01524 812054 www.thegreyhoundhalton.com

HOW TO GET THERE AND PARKING: Halton is 2½ miles north of Lancaster city centre and very close to junction 34 of the M6. Approached on the A683 road from Junction 34 cross over the River Lune using either Halton Bridge at Denny Beck Lane (weight restriction) or the Low Road crossing at Caton. Parking at the Greyhound for patrons. There is some roadside parking in the village on High Road or a small public parking area can be reached along Quarry Road uphill at the little crossroads outside the Greyhound. **Sat nav** LA2 6LZ.

MAP: OS Explorer OL41 Forest of Bowland & Ribblesdale. **Grid ref** SD 502648.

THE WALK

1 Keep the **Greyhound** on the left and follow the main road (**Low Road**) to the mini-roundabout in the centre of the village. Turn left downhill along **Church Brow**, passing the site of the **Old Red Door** pub on the right and some interesting buildings including **Tower House** and **Clock House** on the left. **St Wilfred's Church** is passed on the right. Continue along the pavement on the left-hand side of the road to pass under the M6 bridge.

2 Immediately after passing under the motorway, turn left along a signed footpath beginning at a stile and gate. Cross the stile and walk downhill to the **River Lune** where the new A683 Lancaster bypass crosses over the river. Walk under the new road and continue straight ahead along a track past a sewage works. The track then passes through an old firing range and a military training base and becomes a wide tarmac access road. Keep all the perimeter fences on the right and the path enters a woodland at the riverside edge.

3 The woodland path runs adjacent to gardens and passes under the aqueduct carrying the **Lancaster Canal**. After crossing under the aqueduct, turn immediately right up wooden steps and turn right at a stile up stone steps to reach the towpath of the ornate **Lune Aqueduct**. Turn right and cross it high over the river. On the far side, turn right down stone steps signposted for the River Lune. Turn right at the bottom of the steps then right again walking under the aqueduct following a tarmac cycleway with the river now on the left.

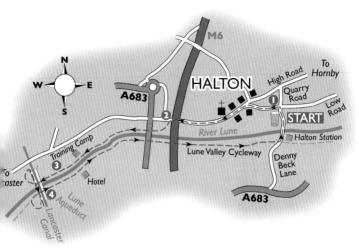

The cycleway is now followed for 1¼ miles upstream, passing a hotel and crossing under the new bypass and the M6, eventually meeting a lane at **Halton Station** where there is a small car park. Cross the lane to have a look at the old station buildings. But to continue the walk follow the lane, **Denny Beck Lane**, down to the river and cross the narrow road bridge. On the other side, follow **Station Road** straight ahead uphill to the crossroads with the Greyhound on the left-hand side.

PLACES OF INTEREST NEARBY

Head down the A683 road to enjoy the numerous attractions of **Lancaster**. Lancashire's historic county town has the **castle**, where the Pendle Witches were imprisoned, and several museums including the **City Museum**, **Maritime Museum** and the **Judge's Lodgings**. It is also easy to hire a bike in Lancaster and try out the many cycleways – up the Lune Valley to Crook o' Lune, along the old railway lines to Glasson and Morecambe, or north along the Lancaster Canal towpath to Carnforth.

The River Wyre

4 Dolphinholme

3.5 miles / 5.6 km

WALK HIGHLIGHTS

The River Wyre is one of Lancashire's major rivers which flows down from the fells. This walk explores part of its banks and follows a short section of the Wyre Way.

THE PUB

The Fleece Inn, LA2 9AQ
☎ 01524 791233 www.fleeceinn.co.uk

THE WALK

1 From the lane crossroads by the **Fleece Inn**, walk uphill along the hedged road (**Anyon Lane**) starting between the inn and the old garage. After half a mile, you reach the village. Follow the road around to the left signed for **Abbeystead**. Follow the pavement on the right-hand side and, when you reach a footpath signpost on the left (indicating paths

HOW TO GET THERE AND PARKING: Dolphinholme is 2 miles east of Junction 33 of the M6 and the A6 at Bay Horse. The Fleece Inn is at the crossroads of Chipping Road and Anyon Lane ½ mile from the village centre. Roadside parking by the Fleece Inn, and the pub has a car park for patrons. **Sat nav** LA2 9AQ.

MAP: OS Explorer OL41 Forest of Bowland & Ribblesdale. **Grid ref** SD 509532.

both left and right), turn right down the driveway leading past **Common Bank Cottages**. At the end of this drive, facing **Common Bank House**, turn left along a tarmac path starting at a bollard.

This runs downhill behind houses to woodland. Just before a lane a 'Wyre Way' signpost is reached signed for '**Street Bridge**'. Turn right along this through woodland with the river on the left. The path runs along a woodland edge and beyond it goes through a gate to enter a field. Walk straight ahead aiming to the left-hand side of the old **Corless Mill**.

Go through the gate on the right by the mill cottage and continue straight ahead along the track leading away from it. Another house is soon passed on the left and, when the track starts to swing right uphill, leave it on the left at a waymarker between two old stone gateposts. Continue along the **Wyre Way** and cross a footbridge over a drain. Go through a gate to enter a field and continue along the riverside. Cross the track to **Wyreside Hall** by a bridge and go through the gate opposite, continuing along the river to reach the road bridge, **Street Bridge**.

Turn left across the road bridge. Follow the lane up to the crossroads by the roadside houses of **Street**. Turn left along **Wagon Road** and follow it for nearly half a mile to the next lane junction, then turn left still following Wagon Road. Pass **Wyreside Hall** and, after passing **Wyreside Cottage** on the right, join the signed footpath on the left-hand side starting at a little footbridge.

Cross the pasture aiming slightly right to a stile on the opposite side. Cross a drain and follow a narrow path between the drain and conifers.

Cross another stile then continue straight ahead to a stile in the wooden fence. Do not follow the tree line in the next field but aim slightly left towards the woodland on the left-hand side of the large field. Aim for the woodland three-quarters of the way along the field to reach a waymarker post leading to a stile into the wood. Look out for the ruined mill chimney in the field on the edge of the wood. Follow the path downhill to meet a lane.

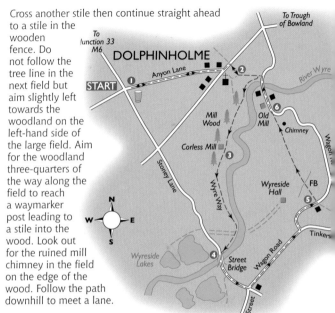

6 Turn left and follow the lane past the old mill. Cross the bridge over the **River Wyre** and, when the lane bends right uphill, leave it on the left at the bollard, joining the tarmac path followed earlier. At **Common Bank House**, turn right to retrace your steps to the village and down **Anyon Lane** back to the Fleece.

PLACES OF INTEREST NEARBY

Head westwards across the M6 to **Glasson Dock**, an interesting village and marina.

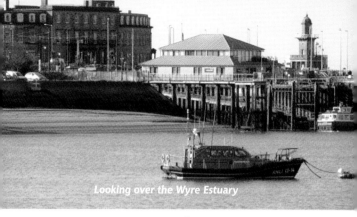

Looking over the Wyre Estuary

5 Knott End-on-Sea

3.5 miles / 5.6 km

WALK HIGHLIGHTS

The Lancashire Coastal Way and the Wyre Way are two long-distance trails that run along the promenade at Knott End. Here there is also a fine statue of a 'matchstalk man and dog', celebrating the artist L.S. Lowry's link with this part of the Fylde coast. He visited here in the 1940s and 1950s to sketch the ferry running across the Wyre estuary to Fleetwood. The walk route crosses the disused route of the Garstang and Knott End railway and ends with spectacular views across Morecambe Bay to the mountains of Lakeland.

THE PUB

The Bourne Arms, FY6 0AB
☎ 01253 810400 www.bournearms.co.uk

THE WALK

Turn left out of the car park entrance to walk to the **Lowry man and dog sculpture** by the ferry jetty. There is a signpost here for the **Lancashire Coastal Way** and **Wyre Way** trails. Turn left at the signpost and follow the promenade between the coastguard station and the **Wyre estuary**.

HOW TO GET THERE AND PARKING: Knott End is at the very end of the B5270 Lancaster Road which begins near Preesall village off the A588 road between Hambleton and Pilling. Follow the signs for Preesall and Knott End and follow the B road all the way to the seafront by the Bourne Arms. There is a large public car park just past the Bourne Arms behind Knott End Café, which overlooks the estuary. **Sat nav** FY6 0BX.

MAP: OS Explorer 296 Lancaster, Morecambe & Fleetwood. **Grid ref** SD 346484.

Pass **Knott End Golf Club** and look across the estuary for a view of **Blackpool Tower**. At the white-painted **Sea Dyke cottage**, turn left following the Wyre Way path signed for **Hackensall Hall**.

2 Turn right along a track directly behind the cottage and follow a path along the right edge of the golf course. Keep to the right of the fairways until a small garage is reached on the right by a waymarker post. Turn left here along the obvious track that crosses the fairway to reach another path signpost at trees. Walk straight ahead along the farm track as it swings left and right to reach Hackensall Hall.

3 Turn left along the driveway leading away from the hall. Ignore the track turning right signposted as the Wyre Way and then the driveway turning left. Just keep going straight ahead along a track (**Whinny Lane**) that soon swings right, then left, becoming a wide track between fields and woodland. The track forks by the entrance signed for **New Heys Farm**. Turn left here and the old railway line is crossed running left to right. Keep to the track which swings right and, after about a quarter of a mile, a gate/kissing gate is reached on the left.

4 Turn left here and go through the kissing gate. Walk to the next gate/kissing gate but do not go straight ahead to the farm. Instead turn left through the kissing gate leading into a conifer woodland. Go straight ahead through the woodland to cross a stile into a field on the opposite side. Continue straight ahead across the field aiming for a stone cross in a gap between the houses. Go through a gate to the right of the war memorial and join a road.

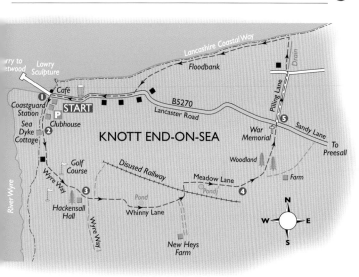

Cross the road and walk straight ahead along signed **Pilling Lane** directly opposite. At the other end go straight ahead across the roundabout and join a signed public footpath on the far side. The path begins alongside a drain next to houses. Walk straight ahead and the path soon crosses an estate road. Follow the tarmac path that runs up to the coastal flood bank. Turn left along it and enjoy the views across the bay. This coastal path is followed for the next mile back to the village and the Bourne Arms.

PLACES OF INTEREST NEARBY

Take the return trip on the little ferry across the mouth of the River Wyre to arrive in the Victorian town of **Fleetwood**. There are plenty of attractions here including the famous indoor market and a fine museum that explores the history of the resort and the port.

The Kenlis Arms

6 Barnacre

3.5 miles / 5.6 km

WALK HIGHLIGHTS

This walk links three transport arteries – the 1790s Lancaster Canal, the Victorian railway, now the West Coast Main Line, and the M6 motorway. The walk also follows a section of the River Calder, winding its way through a picturesque wooded valley from the Bowland fells to its meeting point with the River Wyre.

THE PUB

The Kenlis Arms, PR3 1GD
☎ 01995 603307 www.kenlisarms.co.uk

THE WALK

1 Turn right under the railway bridge and follow the lane to the canal bridge. Turn left and join the **Lancaster Canal** here down the steps away from it. Leave the canal at the second bridge (number 51). Do not

HOW TO GET THERE AND PARKING: There is no actual village at Barnacre, it is the name given to the rural parish south-east of Garstang. The walk starts at the Kenlis Arms, 1 mile east of the B6430 at Bowgreave. From Bowgreave turn along Calder House Lane/Bruna Lane and continue for 1 mile to cross the Lancaster Canal and go under the railway. The pub is on the left-hand side of Ray Lane between the railway and the M6. There is some roadside parking adjacent to the pub. **Sat nav** PR3 1GD.

MAP: OS Explorer OL41 Forest of Bowland & Ribblesdale. **Grid ref** SD 509439.

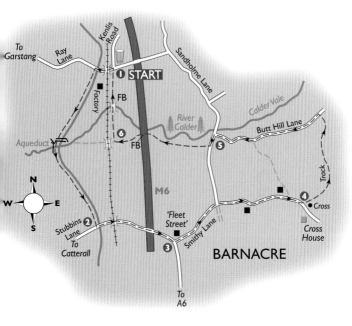

go under this bridge but turn right along the hedged path leading to a lane.

② Turn left along **Stubbins Lane** which crosses the canal and goes under the railway. Pass **Claughton Memorial Hall** on the left to reach a lane junction. The roadside houses here are marked on the OS map as '**Fleet Street**'. Turn left along **Smithy Lane**.

③ Keep to this lane for nearly half a mile to the next lane junction on the right where Smithy Lane bends left. Turn right here following the lane, not the private drive. Follow this lane towards houses for about a third of a mile until a wayside cross is reached on the left.

④ Turn left at the cross and follow the wide track under pylons for half a mile through farmland until it meets a lane. Turn left and follow **Butt Hill Lane** gradually downhill overlooking **Calder Vale**. The **River Calder** soon emerges from the woodland on the right. Follow the lane for half a mile to the next T-junction.

⑤ Turn left along **Sandholme Lane**, only as far as the first track on the right. Turn right along this track (not signed) that begins by a barrier. Go straight ahead and through the small wooden gate between two field gates. The River Calder is on the right but the path follows the hedge/fence line on the left. Follow the field edge to the motorway and then bear right to cross the footbridge.

⑥ Bear slightly left, aiming for the railway underpass. On the other side of the field, do not go through the tunnel but turn right in the same field and follow the field edge with the railway on the left. A stile leads across a footbridge over the River Calder and the path continues ahead through the next field. On the far side the lane is reached next to the Kenlis Arms.

PLACES OF INTEREST NEARBY

Beacon Fell Country Park is a wooded hill with a café and information centre. Here there is a sculpture trail and woodland walks leading to great views of Bowland and west to the Fylde Coast.

The Hodder Valley

7 Newton-in-Bowland

2.75 or 4.75 miles / 4.4 or 7.6 km

WALK HIGHLIGHTS
This walk passes the gothic Knowlmere Manor and a Quaker burial ground. It also traverses an impressive suspension bridge over the River Hodder.

THE PUB
The Parkers Arms, BB7 3DY
☎ 01200 446236 www.parkersarms.co.uk

THE WALK
From the pub walk downhill to cross the **River Hodder**. On the far side, turn right through a kissing gate. Walk ahead and aim for a stile in the opposite left field corner. Cross this and take the right fork, continuing along the steep river bank. Cross further stiles to reach trees on the river bank.

The path climbs away from the river. Cross a drain and a stile in the fence. Aim uphill passing through a gate and then aiming left of a farm (**Farrowfield**). Cross a stile to the left of the farm to join a lane. Turn right and just before the road starts to climb more steeply leave it on

Guide to Lancashire Pub Walks

HOW TO GET THERE AND PARKING: Newton village is 6 miles north of Clitheroe on the B6478 road to Slaidburn. There is some roadside parking near the Parkers Arms and a free public car park nearby. **Sat nav** BB7 3EB (car park).

MAP: OS Explorer OL41 Forest of Bowland & Ribblesdale. **Grid ref** SD 697503.

the right along a footpath signed as a private road. For the shorter walk follow direction 3. For the longer walk, follow direction 4.

3 *For the shorter route*, follow the driveway for ¼ mile until a waymarked stile is reached on the right. Cross this and then another stile and footbridge to cross the suspension bridge. Walk straight ahead uphill through the large field aiming right of the wooded hill. Cross a stile and walk around the right side of the quarried hill. Further stiles and a footbridge lead to a road. Turn right along this only as far as the next stile reached on the left. The walk directions continue from number 8 below.

4 *For the longer route*, follow the driveway straight ahead for about half a mile to reach **Giddy Bridge** over **Birkett Brook**. Fork right on the far side of the bridge along the drive signed as a concessionary footpath. This leads through parkland to **Knowlmere Manor**.

5 Fork left along the track, crossing a cattle grid. It leads to a gate between cottages. Go through the kissing gate and a grassy track leads through another gate keeping a wall on the right and soon reaching a gate/stile in the wall by a concessionary footpath signpost.

6 Cross the wall stile and turn sharp right through a gateway. Follow a line of trees at the top of the hill keeping above the river below. Keep the fence on the left and go through a kissing gate, dropping to the boggy riverbank. Go through another wooden gate and walk straight ahead to the cross the high suspension bridge over the **Hodder**.

7 Turn right along the river. Cross a footbridge, through a gate and keep to the grassy track climbing gradually away from the river to reach a cottage. Go through the green wooden gate in the garden wall and turn

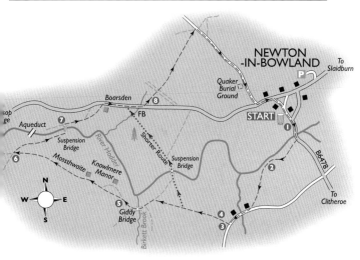

left to reach the road. Turn right and follow the road for nearly half a mile to cross a bridge over a stream and reach a signed footpath on the left.

Cross the stile and bear slightly right to trees. Cross a stile to the right of a ford and follow the left field edge to cross a track and drain. Continue uphill along the left side of a boggy pasture. Aim left of a gate in a wall at the top of the field to reach a ladder stile. Cross this and walk straight ahead along a hawthorn boundary, bearing right at the top of the field to a squeeze stile in a stone gatepost. Cross this and follow the left wall side, crossing another stile to reach a lane. Turn right, following the lane downhill back to a T-junction in **Newton** village. Pass the Quaker burial ground on the right. Turn left along the lane then right for The Parkers Arms or straight on to the car park.

PLACES OF INTEREST NEARBY
Gisburn Forest has numerous cycling trails and is ideal for a family mountain bike adventure. (www.gisburnbiketrails.com).

This part of the River Ribble is locally known as Cromwell's Basin

8 Paythorne
6 miles / 9.6 km

WALK HIGHLIGHTS
The quiet lanes around rural Paythorne lead down to the River Ribble. This is horse riding country and the walk follows a section of the Pennine Bridleway as well as a section of the Ribble Way. The walk passes through the parkland of 18th-century Gisburne Hall and ends at the site of 11th-century Castle Haugh, where once stood a motte and bailey castle. It is thought that Cromwell and his army marched past the castle in 1648 en route from Skipton to camp in the grounds of Gisburne Park.

THE PUB
The Buck Country Pub, BB7 4JD
☎ 01200 445488 www.buckcountrypubpaythorne.co.uk

THE WALK
1 Facing **The Buck** pub, turn right along the lane and follow it straight ahead passing the entrance to a caravan park on the left. Follow the lane (**Settle Lane**) for a further quarter of a mile and, when it bends right, leave it on the left going through a gate signed as a public bridleway. The

HOW TO GET THERE AND PARKING: Paythorne is 2 miles north of Gisburn and is signed off the A682 Gisburn to Hellifield road. There is a parking area alongside Kiln Lane by the public phone box. This is directly opposite the Buck. **Sat nav** BB7 4JD.

MAP: OS Explorer OL41 Forest of Bowland & Ribblesdale. **Grid ref** SD 829518.

hedged track now runs straight ahead crossing several field boundaries, before eventually reaching a gate onto a lane.

Turn left along the lane, which soon bends left. Follow it for about a mile until it meets a side lane on the left. Turn left here along the side lane signed for **Gisburn**. This quiet lane is now followed for 1½ miles. It soon bends sharp right and continues downhill to a T-junction just past farm buildings on the right. Turn left here along the lane signed for **Gisburn**, downhill to woodland and cross a bridge over the **River Ribble**.

After crossing the bridge, leave the lane by going straight ahead along the bridleway for **Gisburne Park**. This follows a track past old houses on the right, bending left uphill as a sunken track through woodland to emerge on a driveway with **Gisburne Park Hospital** over to the left. Follow the **Pennine Bridleway** and walk straight ahead along a fenced driveway. When it forks into two, take the left fork downhill through woodland signed for **Paythorne**. The track crosses a bridge over a stream, **Stock Beck**, to reach a house.

Do not go right to the house but keep left following a track uphill through woodland. It bends left and becomes steeper, turning right to emerge out of the trees as a track between fields. Over a little hill, the track follows a field edge down to the A682 road. Turn left and follow the grassy path along the road verge still following the Pennine Bridleway signs. The path soon leaves the verge to become a fenced path running parallel to the road. The path crosses a stream and follows a right field edge then goes through a gate and climbs gradually uphill aiming for woodland at the top of the hill. Go through more bridle gates to reach the site of **Castle Haugh** on the left.

Go through another gate and continue straight ahead, dropping downhill along a right field edge. The path enters woodland and descends quite steeply to a gate by the road bridge over the river.

5 Turn left across the bridge and then right to follow the lane uphill back to Paythorne.

PLACES OF INTEREST NEARBY

Pendle Heritage Centre is home to a museum exploring the history of the area, a restored 18th-century walled garden and a tea room (www.pendleheritage.co.uk).

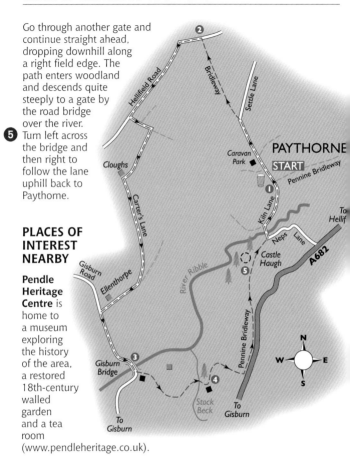

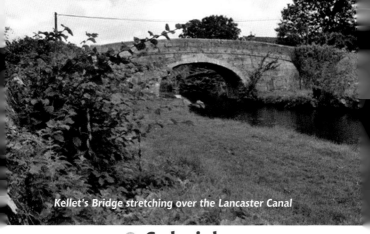

Kellet's Bridge stretching over the Lancaster Canal

9 Salwick

3.75 or 4.75 miles / 6 or 7.6 km

WALK HIGHLIGHTS

The rural Fylde Plain presents a different aspect to Lancashire, flat farmland of ploughed fields and hedged pastures. Meandering its way through this gentler landscape is the Lancaster Canal linking Preston with Kendal. Most of the canal route was open by 1797, to a design by the famous engineer John Rennie, and the canal bridges passed on this walk are historic architectural features. Salwick Wharf, where boats are now moored, once served the nearby market town of Kirkham.

THE PUB

The Hand and Dagger, PR4 0SA
☎ 01772 690306 www.handanddagger.com

THE WALK

Join the **Lancaster Canal** towpath directly opposite the inn by going down the steps next to the road bridge. Do not go under the bridge but turn right along the towpath signed for **Preston** town centre. Follow the towpath for nearly half a mile to arrive at the moorings of **Salwick**

HOW TO GET THERE AND PARKING: Salwick is a hamlet lying 2 miles north of the A583 Blackpool Road between Kirkham and Preston. It is also just south of the M55 and can be reached via Junction 1 or 3 of the motorway. ¾ mile north of Salwick train station is the Hand and Dagger at the crossroads with Treales Road. There is a large parking area by the side of the pub. **Sat nav** PR4 0SA.

MAP: OS Explorer 286 Blackpool & Preston. **Grid ref** SD 464331.

Wharf next to a small car park. Turn right here and leave the canal through the car park to reach the lane (**Station Road**). Cross over to the pavement and turn left. The lane bends right then left. At the left-hand bend, leave it via a signed footpath beginning at a stile in a hedge to the right of a gate.

2 Cross the stile and walk straight ahead through the field to the visible stile on the opposite side at the edge of woodland. Cross this stile and go straight ahead to cross a footbridge in a little copse. Walk straight ahead along the right field edge to reach a gate onto a lane. There is a choice here of a shorter field route (see 3 below) or a longer route along quiet lanes (see 4 below). The lane route may be a good alternative if the fields are boggy!

3 For the shorter field route cross the stile directly opposite and walk along the right field edge. Continue straight ahead along the right-hand side of a woodland to reach a field gate. Go through this then straight ahead between two wooded ponds to reach a stile at the next boundary. Follow the right-hand edge of the next two hedged fields to cross a stile and reach a lane (**Moss Lane East**). Turn right along this and follow it past **Stanley Grange** to reach a T-junction at Point 5.

4 For the longer alternative route along quiet lanes simply turn left along **Treales Road** and follow it for half a mile before turning right along **Jacob's Lane**. Follow this for three quarters of a mile to the first lane junction on the right and turn right along Moss Lane East. Walk along this for a mile to reach a T-junction.

5 Turn left along the lane (**Dagger Road**) and cross the road bridge over the M55. At the next lane junction, turn right along the minor lane (**Salwick Road**) signed for **Catforth**. The lane winds up to **Kellet's Bridge** over the Lancaster Canal. Join the canal here via the gate to the right of the bridge (number 29). Turn right and follow the towpath under the M55. After the motorway, leave the canal at the third bridge passed under. The steps on the right here lead back to the start point.

PLACES OF INTEREST NEARBY

Five miles away is the vibrant city of **Preston**, home of the **Harris Museum and Art Gallery**. The collections include fine art, textiles and coins including a Viking hoard of silver (www.harrismuseum.org.uk).

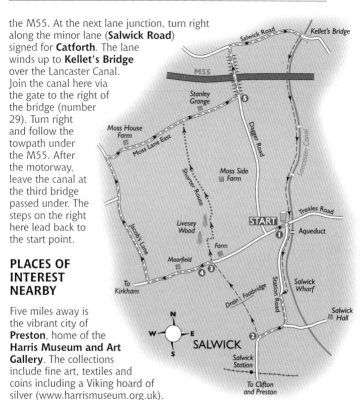

The Roman Bath House

10 Ribchester
5.5 miles / 8.8 km

WALK HIGHLIGHTS
Ribchester was the site of the Roman fort of Bremetennacum, guarding a crossing point of the River Ribble on the road going north to Hadrian's Wall. The walk visits the ruins of an old Roman baths, dating from around AD 100.

THE PUB
The Ribchester Arms, PR3 3ZQ
☎ 01254 820888 www.robinsonsbrewery.com (find it in the pub locator).

THE WALK
1 From the **Ribchester Arms**, cross over the road and turn right along the pavement towards the village. Turn first left along '**Greenside**' past the small car park and war memorial on the left. At the far end, turn left along **Water Street** to the **White Bull** inn. Turn right through the pub

32

HOW TO GET THERE AND PARKING: Ribchester is roughly halfway between Longridge and Clayton-le-Dale on the B6245 road. The Ribchester Arms is situated on the B road at the eastern end of the village. Patrons can park at the pub, alternatively, there is a small car park on the left-hand side of Greenside almost opposite the pub. **Sat nav** PR3 3ZP.

MAP: OS Explorer 287 West Pennine Moors. **Grid ref** SD 652354.

car park then right again along **Church Street**. Turn first left along the lane past the toilets and car park.

When the houses end, the lane swings left then right, passing the entrance to **Lower Alston Farm**. Keep to the private road to **Parsonage Farm** running straight ahead between fields. The access road winds uphill to houses. At the top of the hill, turn left by the cottage then first right along a bridleway through two gateways. Keep near the left field edge and cross the field straight ahead to pass through a gate at the top end. In the next large pasture, bear diagonally left along a faint path heading for the top left field corner. Aim between two woodlands on the far side of the field. Go through a gate to follow an enclosed track to another gate.

Walk straight ahead through a large field keeping left of a copse and pond. On the opposite side, the path drops to a hidden metal gate, not the more obvious stile further right. Go through the gate then straight ahead along the right field edge. Cross a stile at the next boundary then straight ahead to two field gates. Go through the right waymarked gate then straight ahead along the left field edge track to reach **Ox Hey Barn**.

Turn right following the farm road for about three quarters of a mile to a lane junction. Turn left along the adjoining lane and follow this for about 1¼ miles. The lane eventually joins the **Ribble Way** dropping downhill to **Hothersall Lodge** outdoor centre. Continue along the farm road past the entrance to **Hothersall Hall farm**. Look to the left of the farm gateway and a stone head can be seen wedged in the tree. Local legend says this is the petrified head of a devil.

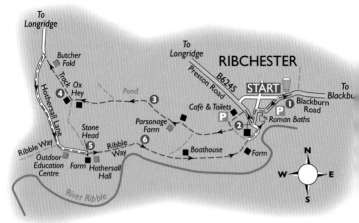

⑤ Continue straight ahead passing Hothersall Hall on the right. Go straight ahead through gates to a ladder stile. Cross this and climb uphill to trees and scrubland on the right with a good view of the **Ribble**. Continue along the edge of the trees and at the woodland corner drop down right to a stile/gate in the bottom left corner of the field.

⑥ Go through the gate and follow the field edge overlooking the river through further gates. The **Ribble Way** is followed back to the village becoming a hedged track leading to a farmyard. Join the end of a residential lane and walk straight ahead past houses. At the wall corner of the primary school, continue straight ahead along the tarmac path overlooking the river. The path leads to a sign for the **Roman Baths**. Turn left up the steps here to visit the Roman site. Go through the gate to the rear of the site to join the lane. Turn right and soon join the road facing the pub.

PLACES OF INTEREST NEARBY

Brockholes Nature Reserve, a 250-acre nature reserve along the River Ribble is great for observing wildlife with bird hides, trails and lakes (www.brockholes.org).

The River Ribble near Brungerley

11 Clitheroe

5.5 miles / 8.8 km

WALK HIGHLIGHTS
The walk follows riverside sections of the Ribble Way through Brungerley Park with its sculpture trail. Real ale fans might also like to visit the traditional hostelry of the New Inn on the return to town.

THE PUB
The Station Bar & Grill, BB7 2EU
☎ 01200 425464 No website, see Facebook page instead

THE WALK
From **Chester Avenue** car park entrance, turn right then left under the railway bridge. Turn right along the pavement passing **Booths** on the right. The road bends left by the **Castle** pub and leads to a mini-roundabout.

At the mini-roundabout turn left following the pavement on the right-hand side of **Parson Lane** opposite the Indian restaurant. Cross over the railway bridge turning first right along **Castle View**. Pass several streets before turning left along **Kirkmoor Road**. Follow this to the end to reach fields and a kissing gate at **Back Commons** cul-de-sac.

HOW TO GET THERE AND PARKING: Clitheroe is signposted off the A59 bypass. In the town follow road signs for Waddington. Turn down Waddington Road then first left along Chester Avenue to reach the car park behind the train station. **Sat nav** BB7 2HR.

MAP: OS Explorer OL41 Forest of Bowland & Ribblesdale. **Grid ref** SD 741421.

3 Do not go through the kissing gate but continue left past houses. Turn right at a stone house along a hedged track leading to a kissing gate. Go through this and immediately turn right through the adjoining kissing gate. Follow the right field edge to the opposite field corner. Ignore the kissing gates but turn left in the same field following the right field edge to another kissing gate. Follow the path straight ahead to a waymarker post overlooking the river and **Waddow Hall**.

4 Turn right at the post to go through a kissing gate and turn right following a path around the edge of the cemetery. This turns left and eventually emerges on the road by the cemetery entrance. Cross the road, turning left downhill. Just before the entrance gates of **Brungerley Park**, turn right along a signed footpath at the entrance to **Park Hill**. Turn left at the wooden field gate and the path runs straight ahead to a kissing gate. Walk straight ahead to the gate on the opposite side of the field.

5 Turn left then right to follow a path running above the river. Turn first left down steps to reach the river then straight ahead past the entrance to **Cross Hill Quarry** to reach an otter sculpture. Turn left downhill at the otter and join a riverside path that leads to a bench. Keep to the riverside path which swings right and follow it all the way to the next road bridge, **Bradford Bridge**. Stone steps to the right of the bridge lead to the road.

6 Turn right following the pavement uphill and go through the gate on the right at the signed entrance to Brungerley Park. Follow the right forking path, and when it forks again at a waymarker post, take the left fork uphill. Keep going uphill and at the path junction turn right to pass a viewpoint indicator. Keep to this path past the point on the left where it was joined earlier. When it forks into two, take the right fork signed '**Ribble Way**' which leads downhill. The path leads back to the road at the lower park gates.

Turn right downhill to the bridge and join the path on the left by the bus stop. Walk straight ahead along the riverside entering woodland. Follow the path uphill via the wooden steps to reach the waymarker post again (4). Retrace the route walked earlier back in the direction of the castle. When the second kissing gate is reached, a shorter route can be taken to Back Commons by going straight ahead through two fields if not too boggy.

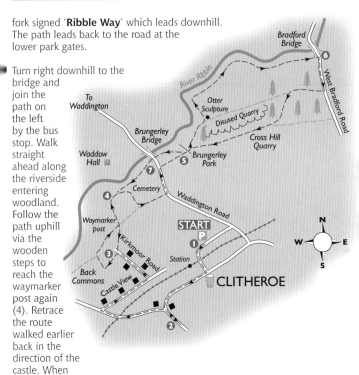

PLACES OF INTEREST NEARBY

Clitheroe Castle and Museum is worth a visit. There are great views and the museum explores the town's history (www.lancashire.gov.uk).

The path leading back to Pleasington at point 6

12 Pleasington

4 miles / 6.4 km

WALK HIGHLIGHTS

There is a memorial dedicated to fell walker Alfred Wainwright on the top of the Yellow Hills which is a fine viewpoint. The Yellow Hills get their name from the yellow flowers of the gorse. The walk also follows a pleasant rural stretch of the River Darwen, a tributary of the River Ribble.

THE PUB

The Railway, BB2 5JE
☎ 01254 207582 www.therailwaypleasington.co.uk

THE WALK

1 With the **Railway** pub on the right, follow the pavement straight ahead through the village. After passing the **Butlers Arms** and the priory, turn immediately right down **Old Hall Lane**. When it forks take the left fork leading to houses. At the gates to **Pleasington Old Hall** turn left up a field access leading to a gate. Cross a stile on top of a wall to the left of the gate. Keep left of a boggy area to emerge at the bottom of a large field sloping uphill.

HOW TO GET THERE AND PARKING: Pleasington village is 3 miles west of Blackburn, on a minor lane off the A674 Preston Old Road. The Railway pub is next to the train station and there is roadside parking on the main street through the village. **Sat nav** BB2 5JE.

MAP: OS Explorer 287 West Pennine Moors. **Grid ref** SD 642261.

Walk straight ahead uphill crossing a ditch and aiming between trees halfway up the field. Aim for the top right corner of the field and a stile eventually comes into view at the woodland edge. Have a breather here and enjoy the view! Cross the stile and walk straight ahead through the trees. Meet a track when the trees end. Turn left along this towards a house but almost immediately turn right off the track following a waymarked path between a wall and trees. Cross a stile in the wall then straight ahead

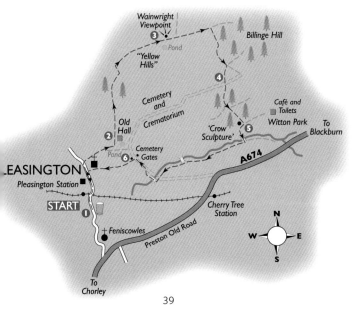

along a right field edge to cross another stile. Keep going straight ahead uphill to reach the **Wainwright Memorial** above rock outcrops.

3 Admire the view from here in all directions. Continue the walk by going straight ahead towards woodland. Cross a stile then straight across a large field to reach a metal kissing gate. Walk into the woodland but then pick up the path turning sharp right. Follow this along the woodland edge and it soon drops downhill, quite steeply in places. Ignore paths forking left. When a crossroads of paths is reached lower down, turn right and the path emerges from the trees through a gateway in the boundary wall to reach a lane.

4 Cross the lane and almost opposite, slightly right, join a bridleway entering a woodland between fields. This path runs gradually downhill and passes through two sets of gates. When the path starts to swing left, look out for a set of wooden steps straight ahead. Go down the steps and continue downhill along the left-hand side of a wooded ravine. At the bottom of the hill, the path reaches the open fields of **Witton Park** next to a crow sculpture.

5 Turn right along the tarmac path which swings left downhill and crosses a bridge over the **River Darwen**. Turn right on the far side of the bridge and follow a riverside path. Ignore the next bridge on the right, a metal tubular footbridge, but continue straight ahead across the edge of the playing field to cross a driveway and reach the next bridge, the old stone **Butlers Bridge**, over the river. Join the driveway again and turn left along it between the playing fields only as far as the white cemetery gates.

6 Turn left here along a path that leads into trees. Turn right at the remains of a gate then straight ahead along a sunken sandy path that runs uphill between fields. At the top of the hill, the path runs alongside the priory to reach the main street. Turn left and follow the pavement back to the Railway pub.

PLACES OF INTEREST NEARBY

The walk passes through **Witton Country Park**, which has a café and children's adventure playgrounds. Nearby is **Blackburn Museum and Art Gallery**, housing various collections.

Dean Clough Reservoir

13 York
3.25 miles / 5.2 km

WALK HIGHLIGHTS
Dean Clough Reservoir is hidden in rolling wooded hills between the rural Ribble Valley and the more urban Calder Valley. The low ridges around the Victorian reservoir, built in the late 1870s to supply water to the local mill towns, provide fine views of these contrasting faces of Lancashire. York village was once the home of the famous Lancashire guidebook writer, Jessica Lofthouse.

THE PUB
The Lord Nelson, BB6 8DU
☎ 01254 246666   www.thelordnelsonlangho.com

THE WALK
From the **Lord Nelson** pub, walk back to the nearby lane crossroads and turn right along the minor unsigned lane (**Old Nab Road**) which climbs uphill and quickly bends sharp left. Leave it at the bend by going straight ahead over the stile next to the footpath signpost. Take the path running diagonally left uphill aiming left of rock outcrops to reach a stile in the fence on the left. Cross this and bear slightly right to the gate/kissing gate in the opposite right corner of the field.

Go through the gate and follow the track downhill towards the reservoir dam. Go straight ahead across the dam to reach the track junction by

HOW TO GET THERE AND PARKING: York village is ½ mile uphill from Langho on the A666 Whalley Road between Blackburn and Whalley. If approaching from the A666, follow York Lane uphill by the mini-roundabouts to the top of the hill. The Lord Nelson is on the adjoining Whalley Old Road, where there is roadside parking. **Sat nav** BB6 8DU.

MAP: OS Explorer 287 West Pennine Moors. **Grid ref** SD 710336.

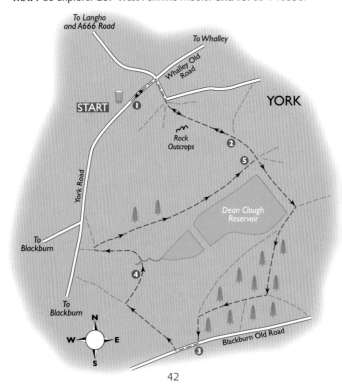

the wall corner on the far side. Turn right here through the gate with the wall on the right, then through the next gate on the left to follow a path climbing uphill to woodland away from the reservoir. The path climbs quite steeply to an adjoining track running left to right through the conifer woodland. Turn right along this wide track, following it all the way to the woodland edge where it meets another track running along the boundary fence. Turn left uphill to go through a kissing gate and reach a road.

Turn right and follow the verge of the road (**Blackburn Old Road**) but only as far as the next footpath on the right signed for **York Road**. Go through the kissing gate here and follow a sunken green track which bends right and passes through a gateway. Keep to this track only for a quarter of a mile until a waymarker post is reached on the right. Turn right here and keep a drain on the left, walking downhill through a rough pasture. The path becomes steeper and drops to a kissing gate and crosses over the inlet to **Dean Clough Reservoir**.

Continue uphill along the obvious path heading towards a hawthorn hedge. The path bears left and goes through a gap between new fences surrounding tree planting. Continue uphill to join a higher track close to a wall and lane. Turn sharp right along this grassy track and it starts to descend gradually back towards the reservoir. It is now followed for three quarters of a mile all the way back to the other end of the reservoir passing woodland on the left. It eventually goes through a gate to meet the track followed earlier running down to the dam.

Turn left uphill and retrace the route followed earlier back to **York village**. Go through the gate at the top of the hill then diagonally left to a stile. Cross this and drop right downhill by the rock outcrops to the stile that leads back down the lane to the Lord Nelson. The panoramic view from the rocks looks north across the Ribble Valley to Bowland.

PLACES OF INTEREST NEARBY

Only a few miles east along the A666 road is **Whalley Abbey**, the ruined 14th-century Cistercian abbey founded by White Monks. This was one of the most important religious sites in medieval Lancashire and the grounds of the abbey are open daily to the public (www.whalleyabbey.org).

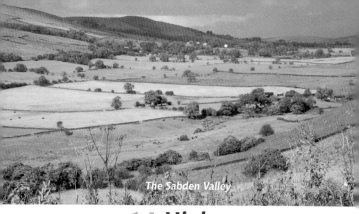

The Sabden Valley

14 Higham

4.5 miles / 7.2 km

WALK HIGHLIGHTS

This walk explores the medieval Forest of Pendle, an area characterised by rolling hills, sunken tracks and narrow winding lanes set against the backdrop of lofty Pendle Hill.

THE PUB

The Four Alls Inn, BB12 9EZ
☎ 01282 778063 www.fourallsinn.co.uk

THE WALK

1 Facing the pub, turn right and follow the main street signed for **Barrowford**. By the wall corner at the village hall, just before the church, turn left up a driveway waymarked as the **Pendle Way**. Keep to the Pendle Way running straight ahead to the right of a stream and entering a large field. Walk straight ahead uphill to cross the top left field boundary. Keep to the left field edge through several fields uphill to reach a lane at a stile/gate.

2 Turn right along the lane and at the next junction turn left uphill (**Haddings Lane**) to reach another junction. Turn right along **Croft Top**

HOW TO GET THERE AND PARKING: Higham village is on the northern side of the A6068 Barrowford Road between Padiham and Fence. There is roadside parking in the village centre. **Sat nav** BB12 9EZ.

MAP: OS Explorer OL21 South Pennines. **Grid ref** SD 808365.

Lane. The lane is followed for about a quarter of a mile until woodland is reached on the right where footpaths are signed on both sides. Turn left up steps to cross a stile. The path goes straight ahead across a field to cross a wall stile on the opposite side.

Aim diagonally left downhill to cross a faint grassy track lower down. Bear right around gorse bushes aiming to the right of a paddock below.

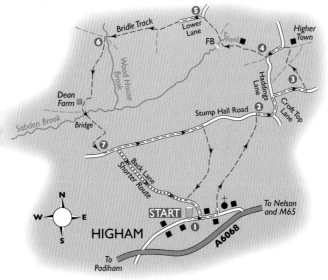

The path drops steeply to cross a stile to the right of the paddock. Turn left along the farm track to reach a lane. Walk straight ahead along the lane only to the next bend.

4 Turn right here along the public bridleway which follows a farm track. Pass an old farmhouse then through a gate to cross a stone bridge at a ford. Ignore the wooden footbridge to the left but aim for a wooden gate to the left of a house, **Old House Farm**. Go through gates and across cobbles to follow a winding track leading to a lane.

5 Turn left along the lane, past a stone cottage on the left, then straight ahead along a sunken path. Pass through another gate and cross a ford at a footpath signpost. Bear right here along the cobbled road and cross another ford by some old outbuildings. Go through the field gate on the far side of the ford then leave the track by immediately swinging left through another gate to reach the stream just forded.

6 Follow the path signed straight ahead keeping the stream down to the left. Walk over a little hill and aim for a stile/gate to the left of the next boundary but not in the field corner. Cross the stile and walk straight ahead through a large field. Cross the wall stile in the field corner by **Dean Farm**, turning right through a gate then left to reach an ornate footpath signpost. Turn left here, crossing over **Sabden Brook**. A track is now followed uphill. After a gate, the track swings right, climbing steeply uphill to reach a lane at the top.

7 Turn left along the lane. At the next lane junction, a quick route back to Higham is to turn right down **Back Lane**. The alternative is to continue straight ahead along the lane for half a mile past farms. After passing a path crossroads at the entrance to **Stump Hall**, continue straight ahead to another path crossroads. Turn right here through a gate along a signed public bridleway. Follow the grassy track downhill, through another gate and follow the left field edge to a gate in the bottom corner. Walk straight ahead to join a driveway. At the lane, turn left to reach the village centre.

PLACES OF INTEREST NEARBY

Nearby is the National Trust's **Gawthorpe Hall**, an Elizabethan manor house which has links with Charlotte Brontë (www.nationaltrust.org.uk).

Grade II listed Spenser's House in Hurstwood built in the 16th century seen at point 6

15 Mereclough

3.5 miles / 5.6 km

WALK HIGHLIGHTS

The Kettledrum Inn is named after a racehorse, Kettledrum, which won the Derby in 1861. This walk passes 17th-century Barcroft Hall and the hamlet of Hurstwood, once the home of Elizabethan poet Edmund Spenser. The walk starts on the Long Causeway, a prehistoric highway and later the main packhorse route over the moors to Yorkshire.

THE PUB

The Kettledrum Inn, BB10 4RG

☎ 01282 416960 www.thekettledruminn.com

THE WALK

From the pub, follow the road signed as the '**Long Causeway**' running downhill. Turn right along **School Lane**. Climb to the next junction and turn right along **Greencliffe Lane**. Turn left along **Red Lees Road** then first right down **Mount Lane**. Follow the pavement downhill for half a mile and turn right at the bottom along **Park Road**.

Pass the Park Road information board overlooking the **River Calder**. Continue straight ahead to the road bridge but do not cross it. Instead

HOW TO GET THERE AND PARKING: Mereclough is 1 mile north of the A646 Burnley Road between Burnley and Holme Chapel. Turn off at Southward Bottom and follow Red Lees Road uphill to the Kettledrum Inn. There is parking at the pub for patrons and roadside parking nearby. **Sat nav** BB10 4RG

MAP: OS Explorer OL21 South Pennines. **Grid ref** SD 873306.

turn right before the bridge along the footpath waymarked as the '**Burnley Way**'. Follow the driveway to **Barcroft Hall** seen ahead. Turn left around the side of the Hall and a stile is reached in the left-hand wall corner.

3 Cross the stile following a grassy path straight ahead uphill. When the path forks, take the right fork aiming for a solitary hawthorn tree at the next wall boundary. The path runs around the right of a hollow to reach an old metal kissing gate in the wall. Go through this and straight ahead across another large field. Bear slightly right until houses come into view over the brow of the hill. Head for the gate leading to the houses.

4 Go through the gate and turn right through another gate. Keep to the driveway past the houses until it bends right. Leave it here via a stile on the left next to a gate and conifers. Turn right and walk across the middle of the field aiming right of houses on the left-hand side. Climb steps and a stile to reach a road. Turn right and almost immediately cross the stile on the left-hand side. The waymarked path leads through gates/stiles to enter the woodland of **Red Lees**. Head downhill and gates lead onto **Salterford Lane**.

5 Turn left aand cross over the **River Brun** to join a footpath at a stile on the right. Follow the path to the far side of the field keeping woodland on the right. Cross a stile at the end, continuing ahead and climbing along the right edge of a steep-sided bank. Cross another stile and go ahead to farm buildings. Turn right through a gate then left through the farmyard to reach **Hurstwood**. The 16th-century **Spenser's House** is on the left.

6 Join the bridleway directly opposite Spenser's House. This track runs

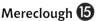
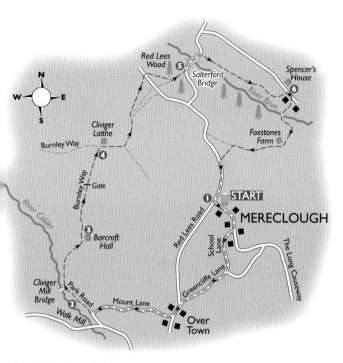

downhill by the side of **Ivy Cottage**. It crosses the **River Brun** then runs uphill to reach **Foxstones Farm**. At the T-junction of tracks turn right along the farm road and join the second signed footpath on the left. Turn left to the Kettledrum Inn.

PLACES OF INTEREST NEARBY

Towneley Hall and Park is the historic seat of the Towneley family. It is a landscaped park with children's play areas, sculpture trails and café as well as a museum and art gallery (www.towneley.org.uk).

Sailing boats moored on the River Douglas

16 Much Hoole

4.6 miles / 7.4 km

WALK HIGHLIGHTS

Much Hoole was a farming village on the old road from Liverpool to Preston and an old milestone can still be seen in the wall close to Th'owd Smithy Inn. Sailing boats moored up on the tidal River Douglas are a reminder that the sea is not too far away. This walk encounters the old line of the West Lancashire Railway that crossed the River Douglas and had a train station at Hoole. The Rufford Branch of the Leeds & Liverpool Canal can also be seen entering the river to provide an outlet to the Ribble Estuary. A walk along the flood bank reveals views to Winter Hill, the moorland source of the River Douglas.

THE PUB

Th'owd Smithy Inn, PR4 4GB
☎ 01772 614844 www.holtpubco.co.uk

THE WALK

1 Follow the pavement of **Liverpool Old Road** away from the pub, past the pub car park on the left. Look out for an old milestone to **Liverpool** in the brick wall on the same side. The road leads to the bypass. Cross the road with care to continue straight ahead down the continuation of Liverpool Old Road on the opposite side. This bends left and rejoins the main carriageway. Turn right and follow it only as far as the footpath signpost and kissing gate on the right on the far side of a stables.

HOW TO GET THERE AND PARKING: Much Hoole village is off the A59 Liverpool Road bypass between Preston and Burscough Bridge. It is signed from the A59 road, turn off by the Indian restaurant along Liverpool Old Road to the village centre. Roadside parking on Liverpool Old Road or Smithy Lane adjacent to Th'owd Smithy Inn and village stores. **Sat nav** PR4 4GB.

MAP: OS Explorer 285 Southport & Chorley. **Grid ref** SD 471229.

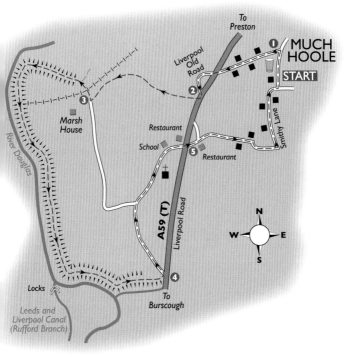

2 Turn right through the gate and the path skirts around the edge of the stables. Follow the left field edge alongside a drain, aiming towards pylons. The path soon goes through a hedge gap and continues straight ahead now with the hedge and drain on the right. The path goes under the first set of pylons and becomes a wide grassy track before crossing under a second line of pylons. At a path junction by gates, turn right through a hedge gap and follow a track with a hedge on the right. This leads to a track junction at the line of an old railway.

3 Cross the old railway line and continue straight ahead at the waymarker post. Climb an embankment and follow the flood bank that leads towards boats moored along the **River Douglas**. The flood bank is now followed straight ahead for 1¼ miles. It passes the site of a railway bridge over the River Douglas and, on the opposite bank, **Tarleton Lock**, where the Rufford branch of the **Leeds & Liverpool Canal** meets the river. After passing the lock, the riverside path turns left and leaves the river, keeping a drain on the right. Cross under pylons again and go through a hedge gap to join the A59 road.

4 Turn left and immediately left down the side lane, a popular truck stop. Keep to the lane as it bends right to reach the quaint **St Michael and All Angels Church**. Continue along the pavement straight ahead past the primary school to arrive back at Liverpool Road by the Indian restaurant.

5 Cross the main road with care and continue down Liverpool Old Road on the opposite side. Pass an Italian restaurant and immediately turn right down **Town Lane**. The lane winds past houses and eventually turns left into **Smithy Lane**. Follow the pavement and when the lane bends right to a T-junction, turn left down the continuation of Smithy Lane to reach Th'owd Smithy Inn on the left.

PLACES OF INTEREST NEARBY

Railway enthusiasts might want to ride on the **West Lancashire Light Railway**, a narrow-gauge steam railway open on Sundays and Bank Holidays during spring/summer and situated at Hesketh Bank (www.westlancsrailway.org).

The disused quarry on Denham Hill seen at point 4

17 Wheelton

5 miles / 8 km

WALK HIGHLIGHTS

This walk explores the Leeds & Liverpool Canal together with a short stretch of the now disused Walton Summit branch of the canal that linked to the port of Preston. The walk also passes the site of the Brindle Workhouse, which once housed over 200 paupers.

THE PUB

The Top Lock, PR6 8LT

☎ 01257 263328 www.thetoplockchorley.co.uk

THE WALK

Cross **Top Lock Bridge** and turn left to join the canal towpath. Follow the towpath for half a mile all the way to the bottom end of **Johnson's Hillock Locks**. Turn right across the canal bridge at the end of the locks. Turn left and left again to join the towpath going under this bridge along the disused **Walton Summit Branch** of the canal. After a quarter of a mile, the towpath meets a lane.

HOW TO GET THERE AND PARKING: Follow signs for Wheelton from the A674 road between Blackburn and Chorley. Follow Kenyon Lane, to the left of the clock tower in the village centre, to reach the Top Lock pub. There is a car park for patrons and roadside parking along Kenyon Lane. **Sat nav** PR6 8EX.

MAP: OS Explorers 285 Southport & Chorley, 286 Blackpool & Preston, 287 West Pennine Moors. **Grid ref** SD 596213.

2 Turn right along the lane and, when it bends right, join a signed footpath on the left between houses. It leads to a stone cottage at the end of a driveway. Turn left in front of the cottage crossing a waymarked stile. Follow the right field edge to cross a stile on the right. The path skirts around a paddock to cross another stile. Turn right and the path runs steeply downhill to a stream under the motorway.

At the stream, cross a stile on the left by the tunnel entrance. Do not go through the tunnel but turn right and cross the stile on the other side of the stream. Follow the left side of the stream, enter woodland and reach a footbridge. Cross this and turn left following a path through scrubland now on the right of the stream to reach a lane. Turn left along **Birchin Lane** past houses. Follow it uphill for about half a mile to reach a T-junction.

Turn right along the lane, climbing gradually uphill for about a quarter of a mile to reach a junction with **Holt Lane**. Turn left here and the lane swings right around the hill to reach the **Denham Hill Quarry** entrance. Turn right into the car park through the kissing gate leading to the disused quarry. Follow the main path left through woodland at the bottom of the quarry. The path soon drops gradually downhill via steps alongside the quarry face and then forks into two. Turn left here to reach a kissing gate at a bridleway sign.

Go through the gate and turn immediately right along the bridleway. It follows a walled grassy track that soon bends right downhill to a gate and farm buildings. Look out here for a plaque in the wall on the left, marking the site of the old **Brindle Workhouse**. Go through the gate, cross a lane and down the farm track almost opposite. When the track turns sharp right, leave it by crossing the stile straight ahead. Follow the left field edge to the opposite field corner. Turn right in the same field still following the left field edge to reach a stile at the next corner.

Cross this stile and turn right, continuing in the same direction gradually downhill through a large field. A stile and gate come into view at the bottom of the field. Cross the stile and footbridge to follow a fenced path uphill to a stile leading onto the canal towpath. Turn right under bridge 85 and the towpath is followed for 1¼ miles back to the moorings at Top Lock Bridge. Leave the canal here by turning left over the bridge. Turn left again for Wheelton village.

PLACES OF INTEREST NEARBY

Astley Park, in nearby Chorley, has landscaped gardens around a 17th-century manor house which houses a museum and art gallery.

Panoramic views from the Haslingden Halo

18 Haslingden

2.5 miles / 4 km

WALK HIGHLIGHTS

This walk takes in the panoramic view from the Halo, erected in 2007 in an old disused quarry on the moors above Rossendale. The quarry produced the famous Haslingden flags used as paving stones throughout the country. The walk follows a section of the 'King's Highway', an old road from Manchester to Clitheroe and a section of the old packhorse road, Watery Lane.

THE PUB

The Griffin Inn, BB4 5AF

☎ 01706 214021 www.rossendalebrewery.co.uk

There is no hot food at the Griffin Inn but there are numerous cafés in the town centre, or the Woolpack pub is a 5-minute drive away.

THE WALK

1 With the **Griffin Inn** on the left, walk downhill along **Hud Rake** past terraced houses. Just before the junction with a lower road on the left is reached, cross over and turn right along a narrow lane, **Clough End**

HOW TO GET THERE AND PARKING: The walk starts at Hud Rake on the eastern moorland edge of Haslingden. Approaching Haslingden from the north, this is signed off the A680 Blackburn Road before the town centre is reached. If approaching from Haslingden, turn right at the crossroads by the Commercial Hotel, following Deardengate and Church Street before turning right into High Street which leads to the Griffin Inn. Park roadside on Hud Rake close to the pub. **Sat nav BB4 5AF.**

MAP: OS Explorer 287 West Pennine Moors. **Grid ref** SD 787238.

Road. This runs straight ahead to reach another road junction. Do not turn left here but go straight ahead across the road continuing gradually uphill. The lane bends right and is joined by a narrow lane on the left next to a field gate.

Turn left along this unsigned narrow lane known as the **King's Highway**, an old north-south road through the **Irwell Valley**. Follow this for a quarter of a mile until it meets a walled track on the right opposite a field gate. This is just before the farm buildings at Acre are reached on the left. Turn right and follow the track (a byway) steeply uphill to a T-junction with a farm road (**Laund Lane**). Turn right, passing farms on the left to reach a lane crossroads by the entrance to a recycling centre.

Go straight ahead here across the lane joining a signed byway. This is **Watery Lane**, an old packhorse road which becomes a narrow path alongside a stream on the left. The path fords the stream – it may be slippery – and then climbs uphill via steps with the stream now on the right. Ignore the track forking right but continue uphill along the walled track that goes over the brow of a hill. The track drops downhill to reach a car park on the right close to a junction of routes.

Turn right past the information board and around the back of the car park. Follow the path running uphill then forking left to the impressive **Halo** sculpture. Walk under it to the path bearing right on the other side of the hill, where there is a good view of **Rossendale** looking south towards Manchester. Continue right, following the path around the hillside with the Halo over to the right. At a path junction, turn right and this leads to a crossroads of paths. Turn left and, at a wall corner, take the left fork through woodland. The path winds right and left to reach a kissing gate on to a lane by the **Top O' Slate** information board. This is marked as the **Lower Entrance** to the Halo site.

5 Turn right and follow the narrow lane (**Cribden End Lane**) which soon bends sharp left downhill. At the track junction and footpath sign, turn left and continue along the lane (**Higher Lane**) downhill to houses and another lane junction. Turn right along **Hud Rake** to return to the Griffin Inn. Alternatively, for the town centre, turn left downhill to join **Church Street** which leads to **Deardengate** and **Manchester Road**.

PLACES OF INTEREST NEARBY

The **East Lancashire Railway** is a popular family attraction a few miles east of Haslingden. From the train station at Haslingden it is possible to take a steam train down the Irwell Valley to Ramsbottom or Bury (www.eastlancsrailway.org.uk).

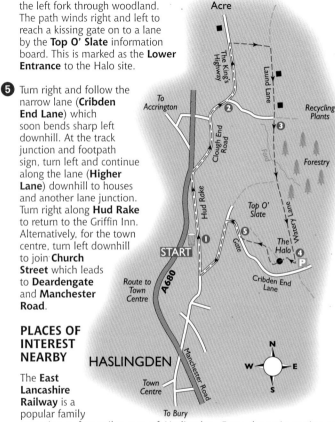

The Leeds and Liverpool Canal

19 Newburgh

4 miles / 6.4 km

WALK HIGHLIGHTS

The Leeds and Liverpool Canal in West Lancashire has a rural character. This walk has views to Parbold Hill and crosses twice one of Lancashire's lesser known rivers, the Tawd. This little river flows north under the canal heading for the River Douglas.

THE PUB

The Red Lion, WN8 7NF
☎ 01257 462336 www.redlionpubnewburghvillage.co.uk

THE WALK

If starting on **Back Lane** outside **Christ Church**, walk back to the main road through the village and turn left along the pavement to reach the **Red Lion** on the left. From the Red Lion, continue along the pavement on the left-hand side of the main road until a signed footpath is reached on the same side next to a house with the name '**Shirleen**'. Turn left here and the path begins at the corner of a field. Walk straight ahead downhill

Guide to Lancashire Pub Walks

HOW TO GET THERE AND PARKING: Newburgh is situated on the A5209 road between Burscough and Standish. There is a car park for patrons at the Red Lion. There is limited roadside parking on the main road and some parking along adjoining Back Lane by the village church. **Sat nav** WN8 7NF.

MAP: OS Explorer 285 Southport & Chorley. **Grid ref** SD 483102.

through the middle of a large field with a view right to **Parbold**. The path is well used and leads to a waymarker post on the opposite field edge.

2 Turn left here and follow the right field edge by the canal. Continue along the edge of large fields, crossing canal bridge 36B over a lane. Continue straight ahead and the path runs along the edge of a garden on the left and meets bridge 36A over another lane. Leave the canal on the left here and go down the grass bank to join the lane. Turn right and follow the lane through the tunnel under the canal. The lane (**Deans Lane**) is now followed for a while. It soon bends sharp left, goes across a level crossing and bends left again at **Tawdside Farm** on the right to cross a lane bridge over the **River Tawd**.

3 Continue along the lane and, when it soon bends right, leave it by going straight ahead along an unsigned narrow lane (**Frog Lane**). This soon leads to another level crossing. Go through the gates and cross the line with care, remembering to stop, look and listen and beware trains! The lane continues straight ahead on the far side of the crossing and after about half a mile reaches a T-junction.

4 Turn right along the adjoining lane (**Hollowford Lane**) following the pavement to the next lane junction. Turn left here along **Moss Brook Lane**. Follow it up to the nearby canal bridge and join the towpath on the right of the bridge via steps. Turn left under the bridge (number 35) and follow the towpath with the water on the right. At bridge 35A the canal crosses the River Tawd again. Pass pretty cottages at the next bridge, crossing the lane to continue along the towpath for another half a mile. Leave the canal at bridge 36A again, this time dropping left down the steps to **Lavender Cottage** before the bridge is crossed.

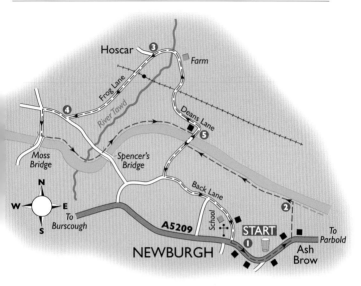

Turn right along the lane and go under the tunnel again. Lanes are now followed back to **Newburgh**. Follow the lane gradually uphill and at the T-junction turn left along Back Lane. Continue straight ahead along this and after about half a mile, it passes the school and church on the right. Return to the Red Lion, walk straight ahead to the main road and turn left.

PLACES OF INTEREST NEARBY

Travel a few miles west to Burscough and visit the important nature reserve of the **Martin Mere Wetland Centre** run by the Wildfowl and Wetlands Trust. It is a great place to spot wildlife, particularly wetland birds and offers walking trails as well as a children's play area and café. The reserve regularly features on BBC's *Autumnwatch* when Martin Mere often enjoys the amazing natural spectacle of thousands of roosting starlings (www.wwt.org.uk).

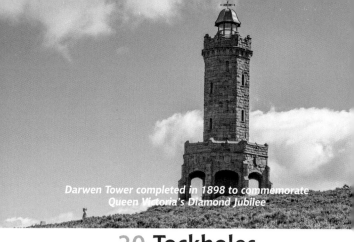
Darwen Tower completed in 1898 to commemorate Queen Victoria's Diamond Jubilee

20 Tockholes

4.3 miles / 6.9 km

WALK HIGHLIGHTS

This walk combines the magnificent views from Darwen Moor with the enchanting wooded valley of the infant River Roddlesworth, known locally as 'Rocky Brook'. The walk climbs to over 1,200ft (375m) and visits the ruins of Hollinshead Hall. Here there is an old well where pilgrims stopped on the way to Whalley Abbey.

THE PUB

The Royal Arms, BB3 0PA
☎ 01254 705373 No website

THE WALK

1 Turn left out of the car park and walk behind the bus stop and turning area. Turn left to the corner of a terraced row and right through the gate next to the first terraced house that leads up a stone track. Follow this uphill to a gate and straight ahead under the trees to face a gate straight ahead onto **Darwen Moor** where the track swings left around the little clough known as **Stepback Brook**.

HOW TO GET THERE AND PARKING: Tockholes is situated along minor lanes 2 miles west of Darwen. It can be approached via the A675 Belmont Road between Abbey Village and Belmont. It is also just south of junctions 3 and 4 of the M65. From the A675 follow Roddlesworth Road to the southern end of the village. There is a car park between the Royal Arms and Vaughn's Country Café. **Sat nav** BB3 0PA.

MAP: OS Explorer 287 West Pennine Moors. **Grid ref** SD 665215.

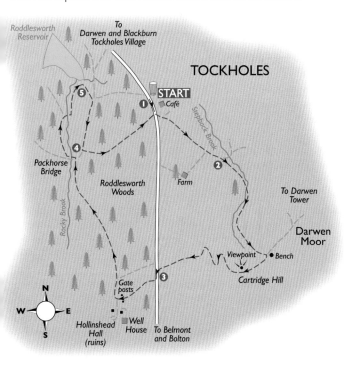

2 Do not cross the brook but go straight ahead through the gate at the Darwen Moor sign. A track now leads uphill with the brook at first to the right. The track climbs steeply, turns right and left, and the stream appears on the right. Follow the track all the way on to the moor to reach a junction of paths by a bench. **Darwen Tower** can be seen over to the left. Turn right on the adjoining track which leads to a gate. Go through this and the track zigzags down the hillside towards the woodland. Walk straight ahead to a gate onto the lane, **Roddlesworth Road**.

3 Cross the lane, turn left and go through a gate in the wall on the right. Walk straight ahead through the woodland and the path drops downhill to reach stone gateposts at the ruins of **Hollinshead Hall**. Explore the ruins and the preserved well house but, to continue the walk, turn right after the gateposts and follow a track uphill to go through a gate. Walk straight on from here following a track dropping downhill to the woodland. Follow it for three quarters of a mile to reach a stone bridge on the left.

4 Turn left across the bridge and immediately right through the metal kissing gate. Drop down steps and follow the woodland path along 'Rocky Brook'. Keep to the path alongside the stream that climbs and drops down wooden steps to reach a bridge over the stream on the right. Cross this and turn left, following a path which soon swings right leading to a bench overlooking the top of the reservoir.

5 Turn right at the bench following a path with your back to the reservoir. This leads to a track junction. Turn right here following the adjoining track straight ahead through the woodland. After about half a mile, the track is joined by a track on the left-hand side. This is just before a gate is reached to the left of the packhorse bridge crossed earlier. Turn left here and the track passes through a glade before climbing up through woodland. Eventually a gate at the edge of the woods leads to the lane. Cross over and turn left to return to the car park.

PLACES OF INTEREST NEARBY

A moorland road from Belmont leads to **Rivington Terraced Gardens** on the slopes below Rivington Pike. The Chinese Gardens were created by Lord Leverhulme in Edwardian times and are slowly being restored.